For: Patti

From: Nancy

Christmas
Date: 2004

I Love You

Debbie Mumm blends together nostalgia, humor, and charm into every wonderful design she creates. This celebrated designer and author loves sharing her kind-hearted vision of the world on hundreds of products enjoyed by people worldwide.

Debbie Mumm

Sisters

DEBBIE MUMM.

www.debbiemumm.com

new seasons™

Having a sister is
like having the best part of
yourself to rely on.

Sisters are nuts
from the same tree.

Having a sister
doubles your wardrobe.

Sisters infuse light
into the shadows
of disappointment.

Sisters offer the honest
opinion you can't get
from anyone else —
even if you haven't
asked for it.

For there is no friend like a sister
in calm or stormy weather.

-CHRISTINA ROSSETTI, "GOBLIN MARKET"-

A sister always
knows when to bring
tissues and when to
bring champagne.

A sister will accompany
you to the candle shop and
smell every fragrance before
selecting the perfect one.

Love comforteth like
sunshine after rain.

-WILLIAM SHAKESPEARE,
VENUS AND ADONIS-

Sisters have the ability
to assure us everything
will be all right.

Jobs, men, and apartments
may come and go,
but sisters are forever.

BLESS the BIRDS

SONGBIRDS

FLY AWAY HOME

Sisters allow you
to experience the joy
of becoming an aunt.

All the brothers were valiant,
and all the sisters virtuous.

-INSCRIPTION ON THE TOMB OF

THE DUCHESS OF NEWCASTLE IN WESTMINSTER ABBEY-

A sister is a source
of strength, wisdom,
comfort, and pride.

Having a sister means
you're bound to get at least
one birthday present
you actually want.

Having a sister
means the
baby~sitter is free!

A sister remembers the
crazy things you did
together as kids
⌐ and won't let
you forget, either!

So much they talk'd,
so very little said.

–CHARLES CHURCHILL, *THE ROSCIAD*–

A sister knows
exactly how to serve
your coffee.

A sister is a
forever friend.

-AMERICAN PROVERB-

Having a sister means
you'll always have someone
who'll split dessert.

BIRTHDAY
TEA

When everyone else
forgets your birthday,
a sister remembers.

When there's trouble in
the love department, a sister
always knows what to do.

When you have a sister,
who needs a hairdresser?

No matter how successful
you become, a sister can still
make you feel like a giggly
10-year-old on the playground.

Sisters are
the fastest road
back home.

When it rains,
sisters will always dance
with you in the puddles.

Leaving home for the first time is hard, but paying the phone bills when you're away from your sister is harder!

A sister's purse
always seems to contain
what you need.

A minist'ring angel
shall my sister be.

-WILLIAM SHAKESPEARE, *HAMLET*-

"I know you
feel for me; I know what
a heart you have."

-JANE AUSTEN, SENSE AND SENSIBILITY-

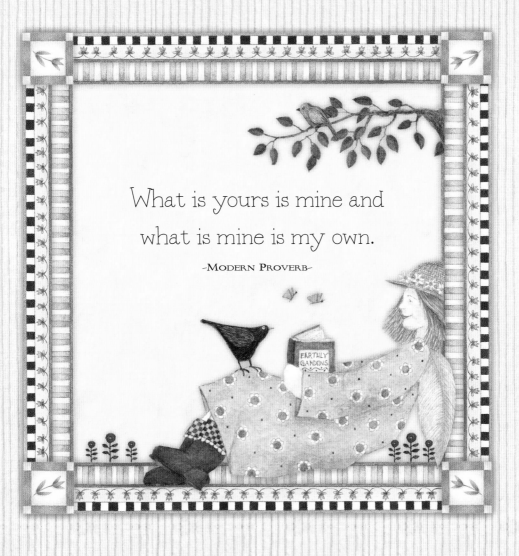

What is yours is mine and
what is mine is my own.

–MODERN PROVERB–

"I do think that families are the most beautiful thing in the world," burst out Jo.

–Louisa May Alcott, Little Women–

When you get one girl you better try two, cause there ain't no telling what one'll do.

-SOUTHERN PROVERB-

Where can one better be than
in the bosom of one's family?

-LYRICS FROM A TRADITIONAL FRENCH SONG-

Even if she dislikes it too,
your sister will defend your
choice of bridesmaid dresses.

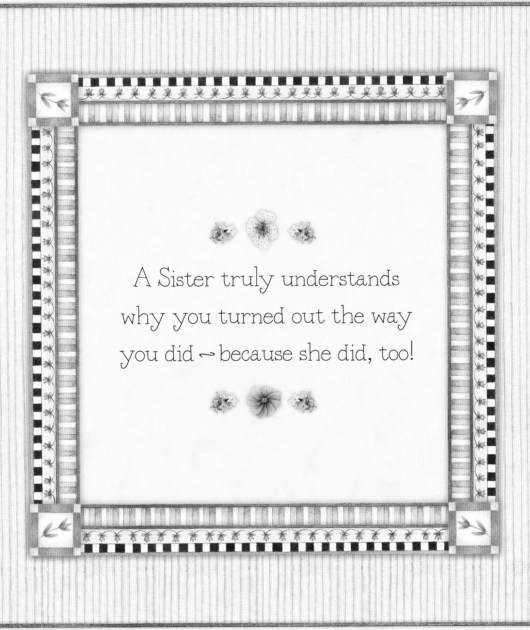

A Sister truly understands
why you turned out the way
you did ⁓ because she did, too!

Having a sister means never
having to do spa nights alone.

Count on your sister
to know your favorite
ice cream flavor.

The older you get,
the more fun it is
to have a sister.

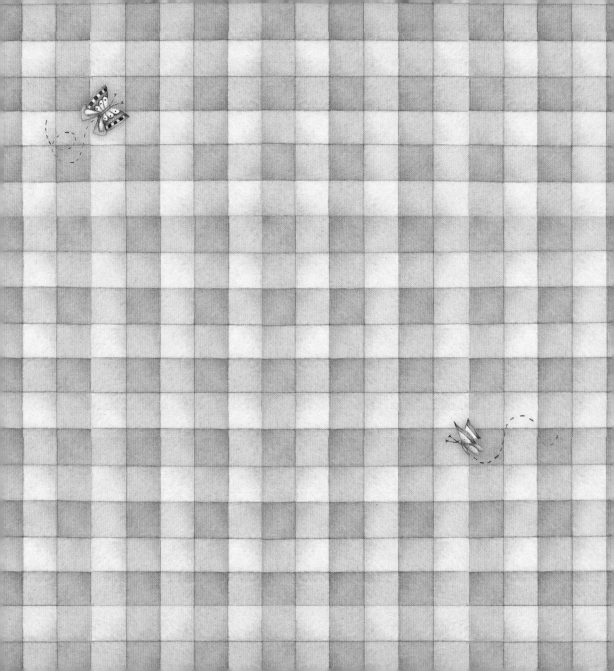